Bear and Squirrel

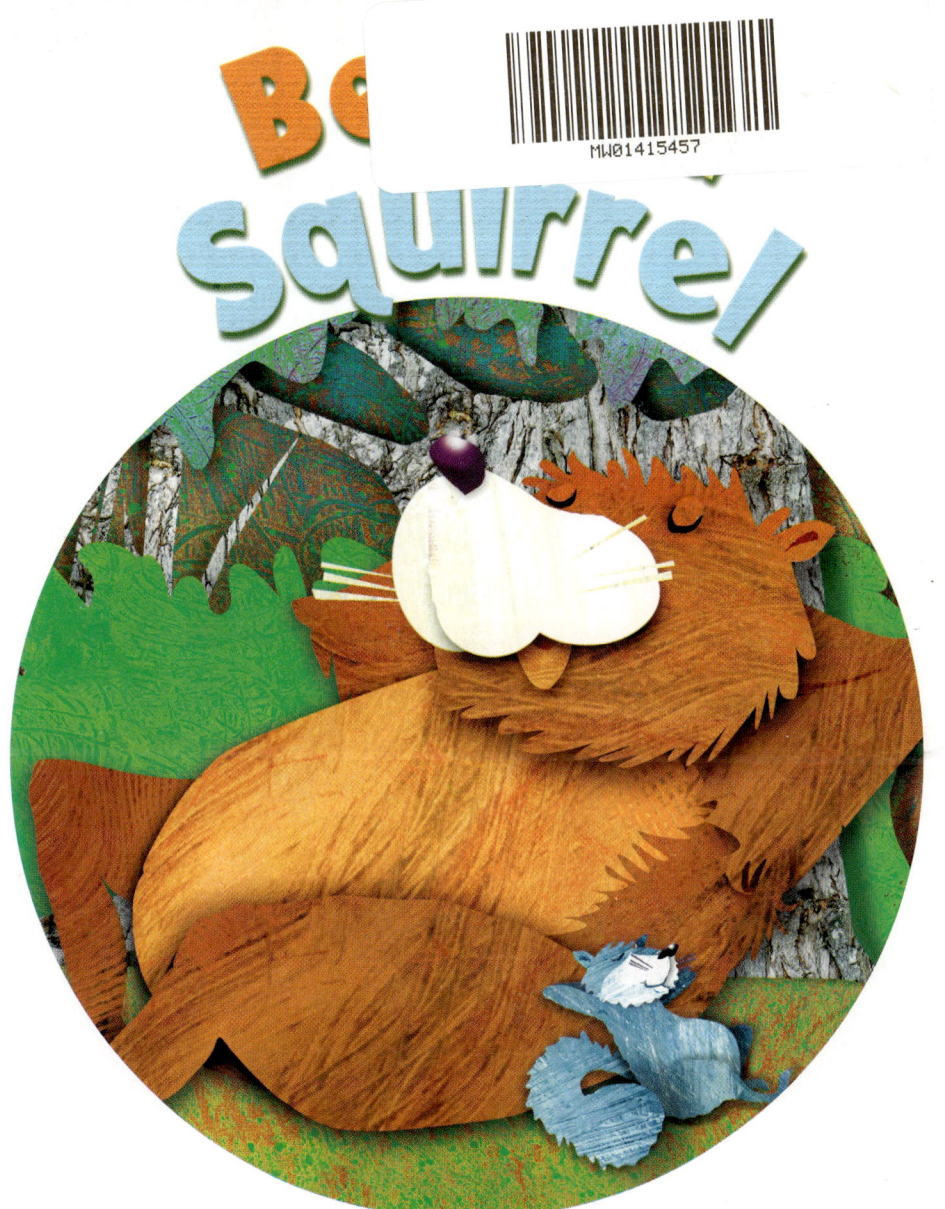

by Gustavo Juana
illustrated by Susan Swan

PEARSON

Glenview, Illinois • Boston, Massachusetts • Mesa, Arizona
Shoreview, Minnesota • Upper Saddle River, New Jersey

Bear and Squirrel met in the forest.
Squirrel had a bushy tail.
Bear had long, sharp claws.
They were both happy to see a friend.

"Hello, Bear."

"Hello, Squirrel. What are you doing in the forest?"

"I am looking for food," said Squirrel.

"Me too," said Bear. "Let's explore the forest together."

Squirrel looked on the ground.
He saw some bugs under the leaves.
"Yum! These bugs taste good."
Squirrel was less hungry than before.
"But, I am still hungry!" said Squirrel.

berry

Bear was lucky.
He saw some berries next to the stream.
"Mmm! I like to eat berries."
Bear was less hungry than before.
"But, I am still hungry!" said Bear.

acorn

Then Squirrel climbed up a tree. High in the tree he found some acorns.
"I love acorns!" said Squirrel.
He ate until his belly was full.

Bear caught a fish in the stream.
His sharp claws helped him catch the fish.
Bear liked to eat fish.
He ate until his belly was full.

After eating, Bear and Squirrel were tired.

They both took a nap.

They slept under a big tree.

Squirrel learned that Bear made a very good pillow!